Ponies

Laura Marsh

NATIONAL GEOGRAPHIC
Washington, D.C.

For Alec

—L.F.M.

Design by Yay Design

Trade Paperback ISBN: 978-1-4263-0849-9
Library Binding ISBN: 978-1-4263-0850-5

Photo credits: Cover, Philip Tull/ Oxford Scientific/ Photolibrary.com; 1, Makarova Viktoria/ Shutterstock; 2, Tim Graham/ The Image Bank/ Getty Images; 4-5, Gallo Images/ Getty Images; 6, Eric Isselée/ Shutterstock; 7 (top left), Ocean/ Corbis; 7 (top right), Image Source/ Corbis; 7 (left center), Mikhail Kondrashov/ iStockphoto.com; 7 (right center), Lenkadan/Shutterstock; 7 (bottom left), Eduard Kyslynskyy/ Shutterstock; 7 (bottom right), Daniel Gale/ Shutterstock; 8, Jane Burton/ naturepl.com; 9, Fionline digitale Bildagentur GmbH/ Alamy; 10-11, Cornelia Doerr/ Photographer's Choice/ Getty Images; 11, ARCO/ naturepl.com; 12 (left), Kristel Richard/ naturepl.com; 12 (right), blickwinkel/ Alamy; 13 (top left), Juniors Bildarchiv/ Alamy; 13 (top right), Rachel Faulise; 13 (bottom left), Foto Grebler/ Alamy; 13 (bottom right), Zuzule/ Shutterstock; 14 (top left), teamtime/ iStockphoto.com; 14 (top right), pastoor/ iStockphoto.com; 14 (bottom left), Andries Oberholzer/ Shutterstock; 14 (bottom right), Matti/ Alamy; 15 (top left), George Clerk/ iStockphoto.com; 15 (top right), enis izgi/ iStockphoto.com; 15 (bottom left), Oshchepkov Dmitry/ Shutterstock; 15 (bottom right), Lagui/ Shutterstock; 16 (left), Geoff du Feu/ Photodisc/ Getty Images; 16 (right), Tim Burrett/ NationalGeographicStock.com; 17 (top left), Frank Lukasseck/ Photographer's Choice/ Getty Images; 17 (top right), Kim Tegg/ National Geographic My Shot; 17 (bottom left), Mikhail Kondrashov "fotomik"/ Alamy; 17 (bottom right), verity johnson/ iStockphoto.com; 18-19, Steve Cicero/ Corbis; 20-21, Flickr RF/ Getty Images; 22, hulton Archive/ Getty Images; 22 (Background), Torkile/ iStockphoto.com; 23, Jack Delano/ Hulton Archive/ Getty Images; 24-25, Westend61/ Getty Images; 25 (top), Dorling Kindersley/ Getty Images; 25 (center), Dorling Kindersley/ Getty Images; 25 25 (bottom), Lynn Johnson/ NationalGeographicStock.com; 26, Medford Taylor/ National Geographic/ Getty Images; 27 (top), Danny Smythe/ iStockphoto.com; 27 (right center), Borodaev/ Shutterstock; 27 (left center), Juniors Bildarchiv/ Alamy; 27 (bottom), Michael Westhoff/ iStock photo.com; 27 (top left), Ben Molyneux Sports/ Alamy; 28 (top), Hugh Threlfall/ Alamy; 28 (center), Dorling Kindersley/ Getty Images; 28 (bottom left), Timothy Large/ Alamy; 28 (bottom right), Dorling Kindersley/ Getty Images; 29, Blue Destiny/ Alamy; 30 (left), Anja Hild/ iStockphoto.com; 30 (right), Iurii Konoval/ iStockphoto.com; 31 (top left), Igum nova Irina/ Shutterstock; 31 (top right), Charles Mann/ iStockphoto.com; 31 (bottom left), jadimages/ Shutterstock; 31 (bottom right), Sian Lewis/ iStockphoto.com; 32 (top left), Rachel Faulise; 32 (top right), Steve Cicero/ Corbis; 32 (bottom left), Jane Burton/ naturepl.com; 32 (bottom right), Ocean/ Corbis

Printed in the United States of America
11/WOR/1

Table of Contents

It's a Pony!

Ponies are special animals. They are beautiful and strong. They are kind and loyal. They like to be around people and other animals.

What Is a Pony?

A pony is a kind of horse.

Horses and ponies are measured in hands. Most pony breeds are 14.2 hands or shorter.

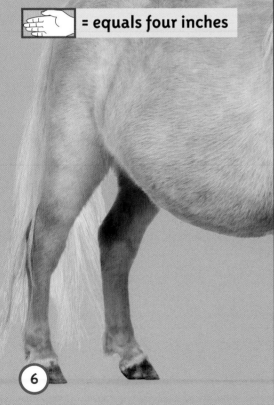

= equals four inches

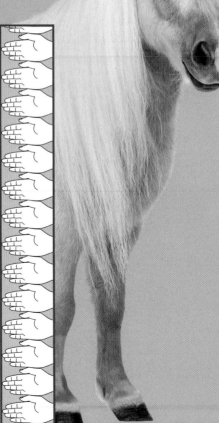

Horse   Pony

L E G S

long legs

short legs

B O D Y

sleek body

wide body

H E I G H T

tall

short

A Foal Is Born!

Pony Word

MARE:
A female horse

It's springtime. A mare gives birth to a baby pony. The baby is called a foal. Welcome, little one!

A foal can stand soon after birth.
It is wobbly on its feet at first.

The foal will run and play before long!

All ponies are called foals in the first year.

Then young female ponies are called fillies.

Young male ponies are called colts.

Pony Breeds

There are many kinds of ponies all over the world.

Some pony breeds have been around for many, many years. Others are newer breeds.

Pony Word

BREED: A group of animals that have similar features and look alike

Section A Welsh Mountain Pony

Exmoor Pony

Dartmoor Pony

Assateague Pony

Connemara Pony

Norwegian Fjord Pony

Colors and Markings

palomino

spotted

blue roan

chestnut

Ponies come in lots of colors.
They can have spotted coats, too.

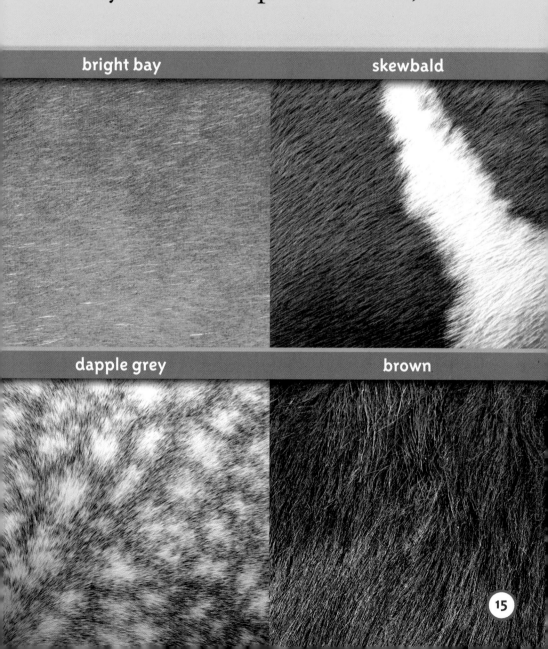

bright bay

skewbald

dapple grey

brown

Some ponies have white patches
of hair. These are called markings.

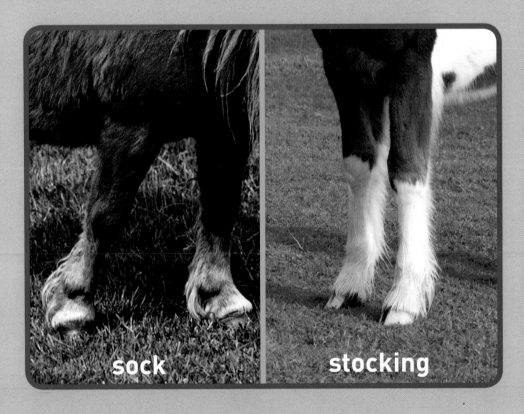

sock   stocking

A pony's feet can have a sock
or stocking.

blaze

star

A pony's head can
have a blaze, a star,
a snip, or a stripe.

snip

stripe

17

Wild Ponies

There are still wild ponies today.

A herd of wild ponies lives in Maryland and Virginia, U.S.A.

They are called the Chincoteague and Assateague ponies.

Chincoteague?
Say *SHING-keh-teeg*

Assateague?
Say *AS-seh-teeg*

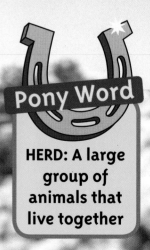

Pony Word

HERD: A large group of animals that live together

The herd has been around for more than 500 years!

Wild ponies are not given food or shelter.

They run free.

Pony Word

SHELTER:
A safe place
that gives
protection from
bad weather

Ponies in the Past

Ponies in the past were used for work.

Ponies pulled carriages around town. They carried people and things.

pony-drawn carriage

coal mine pony

Ponies also worked on farms, in the mountains, and in coal mines.

Ponies Today

Ponies today are still used for work.

But mostly people ride and enjoy them.

People ride ponies in shows and races. They ride ponies on trails.

They even ride them on vacations.

Caring for a Pony

Ponies make great pets.
But they are a lot of work!

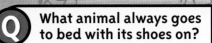

Every day
a pony needs
fresh food and
water, exercise,
brushing,
and cleaning.

Riding

The work is done.
Now it's time to ride!

riding helmet

You will need special
clothes. The clothes
protect you and
the pony.

riding pants called jodhpurs

**Jodhpurs?
Say *JOD-purrs***

gloves

riding boots

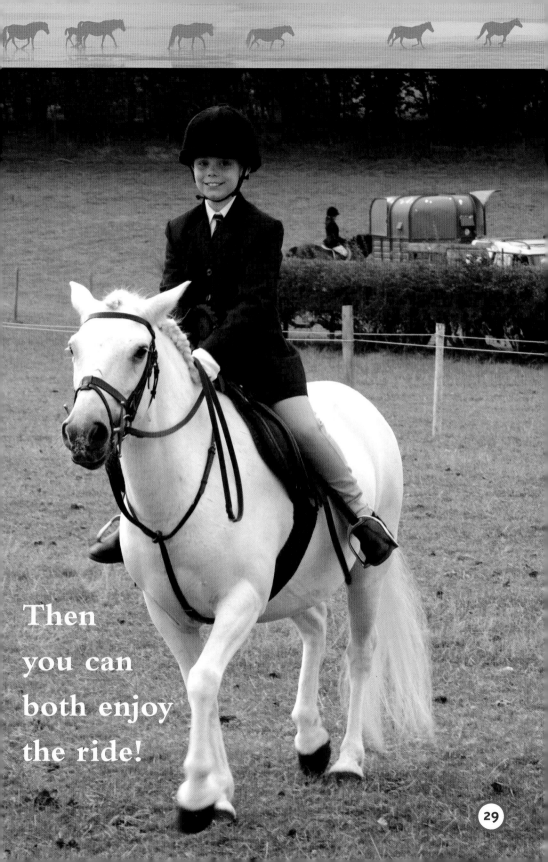

Then
you can
both enjoy
the ride!

What in the World?

These pictures show close-up views of pony things. Use the hints below to figure out what's in the pictures. Answers on page 31.

HINT: This pony marking rhymes with "gaze."

HINT: A pony rider sits here.

WORD BANK

mane   blaze   helmet   saddle   star   foal

3

HINT: A baby pony is called this for the first year.

4

HINT: You need to wear this when you ride.

5

HINT: A pony's neck has this long hair.

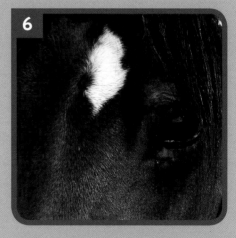

6

HINT: This pony marking rhymes with "car."

BREED: A group of animals that have similar features and look alike

HERD: A large group of animals that live together

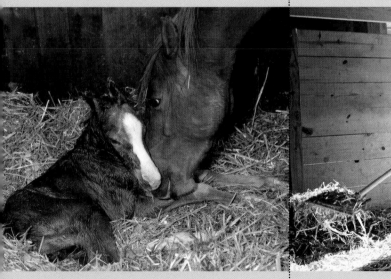

MARE: A female horse

SHELTER: A safe place that gives protection from bad weather